saving the appearances

ahsahta press

The New Series

number 6

saving the appearances

liz waldner

ahsahta press

Boise State University • Boise • Idaho • 2004

Ahsahta Press, Boise State University
Boise, Idaho 83725
http://ahsahtapress.boisestate.edu

Copyright © 2004 by Liz Waldner

Printed in the United States of America
Cover art: "Park, Barcelona" by Kamyar Arasteh
First printing 2004
ISBN 0-916272-79-6

Library of Congress Cataloging-in-Publication Data

Waldner, Liz.
    Saving the appearances / Liz Waldner.
        p. cm. -- (The new series ; no. 6)
    ISBN 0-916272-79-6 (alk. paper)
    I. Title. II. New series (Ahsahta Press) ; no. 6.

    PS3573.A42158S285 2004
    811'.54--dc22
                                    2004004335

FOR KAMIJUN

Contents

i

Mirror 3
Ways, Truths, Lights 4
Representation 6
Sunday, No Peignoir 7
Self Interrogation 8
Granted 10
Leaving 11
Gustatory, Hortatory 12
Post Prandial 13
SweetBee Said 14
Self Extension 15
Adam Au Verso 16
Swimmer, Twin Lakes, NY 18
Wishness 19
Lucked Out 20
Lost Lost Lost 21
Scry 24
Reflection 26

ii

Dark Times 31
Time Lapse Cartography: Synopsis 32
Idiot Song 33

Matters In/Of Fact 35

Eden Tattoo 36

Dis/*coeurs* on the Method 38

Es/chew 40

Yes and No 42

Winter Solstice 43

Apothecaries' Weight: Twenty Brains Make One Scruple 47

Abcedarium, Initial 49

*Miss*ive 53

Of Unknowing, The Cloud 54

Maybe 55

Persian Stanzas 56

Pro(verbial) (Re)creation in the Time of AIDS 57

Exhibits A 58

(Who) Didn't Think Right 59

Varieties of Imperialist Experience 60

What You Don't Know Won't Kill You 63

Saving the Appearances 65

iii

Encode, *Enfilade* 69

Homing In 70

Märchen, Truckin' 75

Queen for a Day 77

Acknowledgments

"Adam Au Verso": *Gargoyle*

"Post Prandial"; "Representation": *The Prose Poem* and *The Gertrude Stein Awards In Innovative American Poetry 1997* (Sun & Moon Press)

"Post Prandial": *The Best of the Prose Poem,* White Pine Press, 2000.

"Apothecaries' Weight: Twenty Brains Make One Scruple": *The Massachusetts Review*

"Self-Interrogation"; "Yes And No": *The Denver Quarterly*

"Wishness"; "Saving the Appearances": *The Colorado Review*

"Leaving": *Salmagundi*

"Swimmer, Twin Lakes, NY": *Five Fingers Review*

"Abecedarium, Initial": *Big Allis*

"Granted"; "Persian Stanzas": *First Intensity*

"Es/chew": *Kenning*

"SweetBee Said": *Key Satch(el)*

"Pro(verbial) (Re)creation In The Time Of AIDS"; "Sunday, No Peignoir"; "Exhibits A"; "Dark Times"; "Of Unknowing, The Cloud"; "Encode, Enfilade"; "*Märchen*, Truckin'"; "The Laundress Maunders II"; "Lost Lost Lost": *The Capilano Review*

"What You Don't Know Won't Kill You": *Luna*

"Scry": *6ix*

"Birthday, New Hampshire, 1993": *Mid-American Review*

"Maybe": *Sentence*

Some of these poems first appeared in *Representation,* a chapbook available from Quayle Press.

Thanks also to The MacDowell Colony and The Massachusetts Cultural Council.

i

...since astronomy has two ends, to save the appearances and to
contemplate the true form of the edifice of the world...
—Kepler, *Epitome of Copernican Astronomy*

Mirror

I do not notice much about myself for other reasons;
This I did not notice for its ubiquity:
I am not too willing to appear.

Ways, Truths, Lights: Leaves of Glass

The sun in wan puddles, pieces
of liquid light like slices
of Wonder Bread. I was born
when such bread was a wonder and built

my body twelve ways. I was twelve
when I moved to Mississippi
and my silence was strengthened
by KKK eyes. Kelloggs,

Battle Creek, *best for you*
in the mornings, in a trailer
tornado of trouble and love gone wrong.
Song? Mockingbird. Listen:

concept of "the catbird seat"
lost on me lost in a sea
of kudzu and crackers. Twenty years after
I learn the lesbians were all

out at the city zoo. Meanwhile,
the wasp slides its slender head
into each cell its yellow legs
like broomstraw embrace. My roomate removes

these nests with a broom
so I don't tell where (between panes

called lights) they are. There are
all kinds of aches, like for Lake

Erie before I wore glasses at six
and clearly saw there was room for me
in the woodpile with the chipmunk
and spiders, under the sink,

and between almost any two leaves:
blueberry and buckeye, sawgrass and blue-eyed.
Wreathes: all sorrows
are the same sorrow, a great tree

with tributary branches and numberless leaves,
like the Mississippi and eventually
its creeks when seen from a plane.
I first flew when I was seventeen

but then I cared more to look at the clouds.
Water might sparkle a sign like speech
and a puddle could give you a shape or a face.
The sky, however, will always be far

enough and empty
a way on through.

Representation

In a bedroom, in any bedroom, in a white room with white curtains, say, on each side of its window like bookends, like bouncers, like the angels with flaming swords at Eden, sit two guys playing guitars. Two guitars. Four women sit in four straight-backed chairs in front of two men with two guitars; that is, they sit facing the window. The curtains billow. The music billows. Notes flutter about the room like moths with no particular star in mind. On the women's faces, the blinds are down. Their worries line them like blinds, like staves. There, occasional notes from one or the other of the two guitars leave a trace like dust from a moth's wing—faint but distinguishable notation. In this way, the women note their songs. In this way, the women compose their faces. In this way, in any bedroom, facing anywhere, everything may be said to depend on who's "their," *whose* their, who's there.

Sunday, No Peignoir

"Much that is hidden shall be revealed" —*Matthew* 10.26

A word, to put a word on the tongue of the morning
that will become my body and blood
in its blue mouth, in its green veins
to run a clear sap between earth and sky

wanting that much
with address of flesh, of bone, to be remodeled
that much to address any world without sin
to wear it well, the mantle of self,

much, that—well—

Self Interrogation

In a box of water in the physics lab, a wave doesn't seem to move what it's in or to be it either, but moves through it, as though it were truly *just passing through*, having figured out how to heed Jesus' injunction to *be in the world but not of it*. But then what is it? It is a thing that keeps asking itself what it is, moving on before it answers itself, not caring by then for an answer. Or it is the look of such a thing.

We called it McCalls Creek although on the map I looked at ten years later it said McCall, McCall Creek. This almost makes my past impossible in the same way also, back there, back then, people said *Woolsworth*, with an 's' in the middle instead of at the end; one of the essential dislocations I suffered was in the incomplete alterity of names. McCalls, then: the shallow, the sandy, the white: Mississippi summer sun on white sand and white kids, its glitter on slow-moving water interrupted by cows and sand bars with their few tufts of weeds like hairs you noticed you'd missed when shaving your shins. The glint of the creek winding around a tree at a bend, a current just enough to sail you by it if the water were deep enough evenly. It never was. Lying on a sandbar just beneath the surface so the moving water slid along my cheeks and I could breathe, I heard a puffing and sat up and saw Melinda floating up from the deep place with a leaf held lengthwise between her lips. A parabolic lip of water went before her. What was the name of that leaf? It is strange to me now how I seem to have accepted everything back then, every loss, every shame, every grief. I succeeded in not knowing there were things to ask back then. Or I succeed in having the look of such a thing.

Granted

Not too free here because intermittent because meanwhile eating with a spoon not made for eating solids but rather for slurping liquids a la Japanese. Here I discover (long pause while I have a thought while chewing—no wonder cows look that way) "look" looks like "bok" as in "bok choy" in my handwriting—why the oriental theme? Am I so suggestible? Is the world, therefore, too? All the soup seasoning is at the bottom. This sounds proverbial but tastes pronominal: it tastes as if *it* were the subject and could taste me. Of course, there is that quantum physics theory that every photon, meon (O Meno, redux), lepton (Leprechaun or leap of faith?), whatever, is conscious.

Which of course is different from having a tongue.

Leaving

That the breath in the trees is so like speech
Means it will mean whatever you feel.
The self becomes the mouth through which
The breath in the trees moves.

All the days, in the mornings, Mrs. A.
Picked mint and washed it.
All the days, the mouth of the house
Shaped the sounds of Farsi.

Gol, a flower.
Sabz, a greenness.
Khaab, sleep.

Today Mrs. A. sleeps in the airport in Paris.
When her plane nears Tehran
She will cover her summer
Clothes with black.

Today the mouth of the house is silent.
Under its tongue, the trees keep *absent*.

Gustatory/Hortatory

Fine Dining, I thought, complete with capital letters. It is 8:06 in the morning, not the hour to think of fine dining, one would think, not the time to find it in one's mind like a strange hat found on one's kitchen chair at 3:27 in the afternoon, goodness, exclamatory, whence—and yet petted on the head and given a place at the table because found there. Oh the head of the table, the last supper, M. Prevert, prix fixe, meal prepared; to be dished and dissed, a plate like a halo behind yr head, soon to be hors d'oeuvre for the faithful even as behind your back the project progresses: make mincemeat out of, and hence back to dining, if not fine. Finely chopped, but the stuff in jars always looks like bruises. Not so fine. Fines for littering, fines for loitering, fines for beating your wife to a pulp (oj). Mighty fine shine on ten silver pieces, a shekel, a bushel, sorghum, spelt, wheat. W h e a t, I thought, like so. 8:13 a.m., ante meridian, Latin on the tongue every day and who notes it? The placebo effect: I place the wafer on your tongue, my meaning in your mouth, we mostly think we know what one another is talking about. We are mostly wrong. Two people cannot eat the same food, held up as a profound thought. Personally, I do not find this lonely or even particularly true, since what does a baby at the breast do but eat, eventually, what you do? Or, whenever you like, eat a leaf of lettuce and eat light of days it ate. Shine Dining. This light on the sheet, that on bare foot, this other that makes the numbers 8 and 1 and 6; this that moves me to pen before breakfast, and that bidding, don't think capital P, just put it down and eat.

Post Prandial

—for SweetBee Smoothfield

Time, fine, a fine time was had by all. The tine of the fork, the fork of the tree, the tree of life, the life of Reilly and now it's either Irish or smiley. Eyes, nays, *pince nez*, sweat bee. A sweat bee reconnoitering me. The cicada sound swells and dies like the sea on the sand, like the breeze in the trees. The bee's still reconnoitering me. An orange-edged winged thing flies by fast. The band about my brain tightens. The buzz saw, the band saw, song of some bug, and the sweat bee lands on my blue muu-muu, probes to be sure it's missing nothing sweet. Its eyes attuned to another frequency, it can't be sure. Me, neither. SweetBee, hello, I am fickle. Something stung me at yesterday evening's dinner party. It left a welt like missing you.

SweetBee Said

SweetBee said it's nice to appear
with a spine now and then.
By this she meant to congratulate x
on appearing in print. Print
was the only way x <u>could</u> appear; otherwise
she was just the blank shapes
between letters, the silence
between words, conditions
not generally thought of as spiny
or even particularly noticeable—
rather, the outward, inaudible signs
of absence. It's a problem, no matter
what form you appear under.

Oh but SweetBee, attuned to
the magnetic petals of the sun, knew
what it was to be drawn into being and so
danced out words, drumming the air,
each gesture sketching the signs
of an electro-magnetic spelling bee. X,
listening, appeared
and disappeared
in a Morse code of being.

In the beginning was the wing of the bee.
At the end of desire, the word made flesh.
In between, the sweet honey
of the language self.

Self Extension

The little boy in the purple shirt walks his wheelbarrow, looking. The tines of the pitch fork chatter on the orange metal, their curve like bones. He is young to be doing such work. His family is missionary. They labor together outdoors all day.

He gives me no idea, the boy. The orange is good against June green. But each word will call to certain others; certain words allow (me) to be.

A certain sensibility seated next to some universal grammar; a sensitivity to the seating chart's possibilities: the hostess with the mostest melts on her guest's tongue.

(Here, a gust(o) of breath...)

I am a guest in this country. Language bids me sit and eat. Writing is being read like sex is in the head. Wherever two or three are gathered in my name, there am I, Jesus said. The worker's tools are an extension of his body, said Marx. The pitchfork's tines do curve like ribs. And the helpmeet created where 'eye' meets 'earth'?

God is the production of syntax.

Adam Au Verso

He is holding his chin in a thoughtful way while he sleeps.
It is a good thing he is not a pipe smoker; the pose would
be too much. Birds are whistling up the hot day to come
through the window for my left ear. I let him be thinking
about these. "About" spatially, all about, like seeds scattered
about the thistle and the mind a finch. No. Like clouds close
about the treeline and the few checkmarks of swallows
speckling the sky. More so. Thought the pebble, widening
rings of water into feeling, the peculiar circular melancholy
of the downward spiraling song of that bird I first heard in
the woods in the middle of Peak's Island, Maine, that you
go through to get from the ferry side which is the city side
to the other, craggy ocean side. I lived there alone, Maine. I
decided to call it a thrush, a word full enough in the throat
to matter. Matter, a transitive and intransitive word. Thrush,
throat, hoof and mouth, the toenails of strangers. Bleh. There
are horribles, yes. There are also the songlines the thoughts
travel, singing the world up out of its sleep, "its", the mind's,
too, mine. Opals, eyes with cataracts and glimmers, mother
of pearl excited to brilliance—his eyes flutter and almost
open and I smile, it is so like a cartoon. In the beginning
was life and then Looney Tunes, only in 1964 I didn't know
it came in that order, I was being raised up as a vegetable,
the sun grabbed my petals and pulled, I had nothing to do
with it, I thought that that cartoon music while a pig shoots
a rabbit and the sun has little arms coming out of its face
near its ears that it rubs its eyes with were without reference

and, so, everything. And not funny. I had no reference. Nor had God. But thirty years later, his eyelids flutter. He rubs his eyes with both fists and the world begins. I imagine I could have been a child, I imagine his mother upstairs was mine. Am I making another cartoon? A songline is drawn: one brow twitches, an especially quickening sparrow sings. Matters: the sleeper's elbow and knee almost meet. Out the window, the dead neighbor's lawn burro stands, confronting a little dead bush. But I must keep my eye on the sleeper who narrates with gesture and breath the world he lets be made from his sleep. A pale blue sheet covers his ribs.

Swimmer, Twin Lakes, NY

Churned water silver green, the arm churning paler still. The trees a green cloud at the rounding end of the world the arm is reaching for. Chalice: the hands cup, the body moves. How the words "the body" become weighty, the silver heavy in the hands. How the grail glows pale on panels in oils gone dark with varnish of day and day. The wine that is yet untasted dreams, wine-dark dreams of the painter's lips. The lip of the cup that rounds the liquid rounds the world. The far shore, the arc of the mouth. The body moves, is moved through language; tastes itself on the wor(l)d's lips.

Wishness

There is this wish, that wish, and the other wish.

There is the wish not
to feel this way.

There is the wish in the heart
of the geranium leaf
such that where the leaf is lighter,
its shadow is darker.

There is the wish on the part
of my hair that fell in an arc
to have fallen in a circle
that it might be connected still.

There is the wish to be born.

There is the wish to be known,
and there is the wish to be known.

Lucked Out

Cat whiskers the grass.
Put the closed door inside the mown meadow,
Let the trees be what is known of gates,
The wind of hinges.

Right over the trees the sky is shirt color, his,
Then his eyelashes black as a beetle's legs
So eye becomes the whole body,
Meadow the carapace and motive:
What sniffs the white cat through the morning
And makes the green to open
To eat sun and 'if' and 'is'
And love.

Lost Lost Lost

...for whosoever would save his life shall lose it... —Luke 9.24

i. Lost sheep

I don't know where I am to be found.

I know *the way to a place is called direction;*
truly, *knowing is not enough.*
And in what sense am I a place?
Hearing wants to be nominated—
the bee hears the sun's electric song
and sings along by seeking.
Why argue this?
But touch insists on its place at the table:
in green pastures make me to lie
down and eat of the green
body, until I am found enough
to be my own bourne

and like a seed, saved.

ii. Lost coin

I feel sheepish. I buried the money
(mercury-winged) knowing exactly
where in earth my cache of silver
coins lies: that it loses itself
to save itself
simply isn't true.

iii. Lost daughter

Some days my feeling is wanting
to find something. I am waiting
all the days to receive this communion.
The sun's coin on my tongue is a token:
the day spends itself on journeys of words
and buys me a ticket to days I will lose.
The sun travels its shadows. I don't move.

Day speaks to day with my tongue;
it traces across the pasture
fir, birch: letters that spell out my name,
this *address of flesh* the same,
a green grown of ten thousand lost things.
Tonight I will lie in their shadows,
the better not to be found.

Scry

*

The candle makes a little pool of itself
almost black, the wax meaning

the black feeling there are no stays,
the structure of days frail

really, no one, no thing
no where to go.

Looking is a cold black pond.
Under is not better but then you belong.

*

The reflection of its own flame
casts a moon on its waters.

What will rise
to such a bait?

In such a bright mirror
I see my face. It peers

into my face and then my face
disappears

in a brimming
and a thin stream of wax running,

what I looked for become,
unlooked for, a wing.

Of wax. Bees' wax.
Flowers were there, and the bees' dance.

The wings' figures in air signify
something to go to is there.

*

A pattern tells you where.
Someone tell me.

What wings to read to know.
Where. How to go.

Reflection

Wary, I sit down,
push papers around,
pick up my pen.

Writing Pins
they were called in Mississippi
to distinguish from pins
that prick or stick things together.

No distinction, to speak of, really.

To speak of: tongues of flame.
The candle growing itself an angel
wing out of the heat between
head and body. I'd prefer angels have only
one wing, patterned after the unicorn,
the better to defy the laws of physics
and be miraculous.
However, I acknowledge every necessity
is a mystery and anyway,
I invented this reason
for my desire to give it a name.

What if we all had heads like flames?
What if we do, nodding and trailing smoke
in the wake of one another's thoughts,
ideas interpolate?

In 1487, Firenze, Fra Pietro Ponzio
wished for a glass of hock.
His wish wings me here, late
in the holiday season, wishing
for you in the woods of New Hampshire
tonight. I'm—well, not
particularly moved by this thought.
Here's where wariness comes in,
stage left, late. My Writing Pin
is eating at me who earlier ate
of cheesecake a bite, of pretzel a few,
of pear a whole, of pistachio, many.
My heart is stuck, I'm perforate:
the pin came loose; I lost you.
How many pens can dance on the head
of an angel without a wing? Plenty.
Poor Writing Pin without a wing
but with the prayer, will a fourteenth year
in the wake of *address unknown* last you?
Caring anymore is a habit, virtually.

Penned in. Put out. I have no idea how
to get somewhere from here.
An untoward accent over a vowel?
A mirror?

ii

Does God ever judge us by appearances? I suspect that he does.
—W. H. Auden

Dark Times

The flickering shadows of leaves.
The prayer of a fly with red eyes.

The star chart made of a leaf by a worm.
With a mandate from heaven in its heart.

The archaic song *Continuo*
Percolates through the throats of birds.

The plant spines curved in arcs like sun's.
The sun swung leaves by stems.

The glimmer of water in candle basin
Registering presence with sky and eye.

Deduce.

Let the syrinx song.
The star shadow.

Time Lapse Cartography: Synopsis

In the blank skies over Europe, there are no words but inside each blank country's color floats a word, its name. A milk jug bobs on the face of the waters, the clock face rests in sleep. At the beach, a shoe. In the dunes, a woman. The three grains of sand on her skin, the skin between her fingers spread. A shadow: overhead, the villagers peer in. Grain, grain, time. The wrinkle grows from mouth to nose, the shadow lengthens, the planet spins. Colors bleed. Czechoslovakia, name without a country. Yugoslavia, white fills in.

Idiot Song

If I call it, will it come to me? —"The Idiot's Song," Rilke

We are in Sarajevo
doing waiting for Godot

salvate volvo,
great momo!

When I was there I was 18
I was 18 outside Dubrovnik
looking at sink holes, swallets
blind rivers, every given
of Karst topography and guess what
I'm afraid so
I wanted to die

I remember a gas station
I remember a white dust
I remember how it felt to sleep
alone—poor me

This: that being what it is,
Dependent on its being for water,
limestone features the very thing
that will cause it when it rains
to be eaten away

No river can be blind to me
When anyone goes below, I know

where they go
no wanting
no waiting
no *no*

Who thinks a shadow entails a sun?
sub sole—they die and die

It when it rains
I when I
That wanting itself was the rabbit's hole
cipher that saved me

place saved
flight out booked
room in supply line for a *me*

I waited a long time
in varied (ter)rains,
nobody eating me but me

Waiting for Godot in Sarajevo,
let them eat faith:
clap your hands if you believe
Alice *uber alles.*

Matters In/Of Fact

The bumblebees are dueling, trioling. It is alarming. Now and then, a clump of buzz swoops down on me. In between now and then, the buzz is invisible, and above.

The wasps are gnawing the deck table. They like the end in the new sun best. Wet and weathered must make the best nest.

Lots of largish gnat-type things flail through the air around me. Hurrah, I am not Hieronymous Bosch. Maybe it's my magnetic field moves them like iron filings, maybe in a pattern one with a fingernail bigger than a tree could see.

A tree could see bird calls to be wending the waves of grasses, could see the bugs tying electrical bows around me, an offering to their gods. Their god of—what god would like me in my new white socks and my 1950's seagreen raffia Portuguese church rummage sale earrings?

All the day long, I fought to be here, left three fingers curled around pen cap, finger and thumb cradle the notebook spine. What did I fight? Say the tool box, the planter box, the top soil, nasturtium seeds. Say the scouring pad, the grocery store, the recycling pile, the sick geranium. Say the boxes of clothes and books and soaps and prescriptions. Say the thing that is here that could be better there. Say the thing in me still certain it is sin for me to be.

Yet the sky is air for me to breathe. And I am here.

Eden Tattoo

After I read it, I said
I didn't want to know that.
In a list of terrible tortures
one in particular so appalls
I know I will never unknow it;
it, after all, has me down pat.

It went right to its place in me,
lock implying a key
like *The Night Porter*, a movie
someone like me doesn't need to see—
I had a private screening.

I hope I thought his poem would redeem his
list of terrible tortures.
Sappho said you shouldn't prod
the wrack on the beach if you're squeamish.
I did, yet I am, unlike god.

Last month I lay on the bathroom floor
having sliced the side of my finger off,
a flood of blood fountaining out,
afraid if I fainted as usual, I'd die.
Now I turned the page for more.

That's *how* it happens, not why.
An object of violence is remade a thing
cast out from a suffering self like ballast.
Every new violence has access,
a key that fits the poor body's lock,

the mind only another orifice,
a keyhole that can't be blocked,
pricked out in permanent dye.
But why? I hope
it's nothing to do with knowing

which has everything to do with desire.

Dis/*coeurs* on the Method

An awful lot of things are busy. A spider egg thing is throttled by the breeze and the spider bite on my wrist vein swells and makes a tiny golden seed. I am not sure what the bumblebees mean, dragging their shadows over the barn wall's computer screen. I live in the barn, and behind the blind of the bathroom window, the buzz can be sudden and too near for outside. As with words, a lot of the outside is inside in there.

What was yard hasn't been mown in months. Tall grasses move the way I crave to move with you through the no-thing sex makes. There is also how the breeze feels in my sick ear and how the light goes through the maple noses here. Wasps sail trailing their legs behind like cripples with wings and find a wall and fly right in. The sun sears the windshield, shifts and slits sharp so fits of dark light burn into my brain.

What really can come in? The light is an electrochemical twitch, rod and cone, radio retina: *Come in, home.* The catbird call and the chainsaw whine flutter some drum. A wave moves through the inner ear sea and the sounds of the things of this world come to be. The doves inside the sand dollar are a skeletal olive branch the ocean offers me. The spider spit in my wrist, the grit in the oyster fruit, seed and flower at once. Goethe's analysis of the parts of plants: this becomes this becomes this: the thought of the body a figure of speech: "I want" one way to say the grass, the spider biting, my busyness. Say some others, but not the heart.

Es/chew

The better to hear
you with, my dear.

Come right
in, prayer.

Let those who have ears to hear, hear.
(Ab. Sourd, bien sûr.)

Of course, of course.
Amo, amas:

He listens.
She glistens.

Dear god, don't
let me use.

Shadows wave. Wane.
Weather, and in that vein,

a work of translation:
shoot up. Get high.

Plough the clouds.
Sky furrows, the brow

of night, an evil
thought, a star

especially bright:
anger, just that.

Scat, track, shit, horse
and what'd he just throw in our yard?

Of night, a needle.
Erose, the petal

of the rosary to ring
god's words around.

Erose, those words
in the mouth of night

where no teeth
are.

Yes and No

Exactly the problem is
no nightfall of a day past is
here and I have to be here with what is.

Here the poinsettia dies
or at least that's what
losing its leaves looks like.

My heart still skips its beats.
I want a hand to feel my ribs
and like them and what's underneath.

A hand not mine.
A hand not Adam's.
Not God's whose hurts.

The sky is the color of last light on water.
Too much silver. My back hurts.
Trees out the window, too still.

Exactly the problem is
I have to make it up as

I go and I've never believed there was
Any *where to go*.

Forgive so you can go on loving.
The light like an exhalation declines.

Winter Solstice

i.
Watchman, what of the night?

The wall plugs have perfect mouths.
They look to be full of dismay.
They're plugged through their eyes
into virtual realities:
virtual humidifier, virtual lamp.
PureMist (copyright) and GE (light):
Let there be amps, joules and watts
on even the darkest day.

The watchman said,
the morning cometh, and also the night.

In the beginning was electricity
soon followed by urban decay.

ii.
If ye will inquire, inquire ye:
turn ye, come.

A Pelikan ink bottle squats
by my birthday bottle of burgundy.
There's more wine than ink.
This sounds like Words To Live By,
a suitable subject for inquiry,
but pardon me, it's too late to think.
Besides, the candle now leans on its wing
and when a wing becomes a crutch,
it's time for angels anonymous.
O wise men of Haddam,
our shopping days are numbered.
From credit checks we learn
belief is a terrible thing
to waste. It leaves a taste,
and water stains that after midnight
turn to wine and stink.
Please, no messy miracles
or gifts we can't return.
If a stranger asks you for your coat,
give him your sweater, too.
If you don't know a stranger,
dress for two. Hence, the dress
code of the anorexic, who

tastes virtually nothing but belief,
is legalistic as Leviticus.
Their perfect mouths are full of mind
lest nothing them dismay.
I use the stem of a poinsettia leaf
to right the candle wick and worry
this is cruel. It's a yellow leaf
and so's the flame, but who's
this congruence a comfort to?
Sing praises to his or her name.
The days grow longer and get colder.
Since yesterday, I'm a year older.
The night sky is a virtual mouth of ink
into which day will dip her pen
and so begin again to write
us the letters of our names.
Gender-bending deities
into the publishing game.

iii.
The heavens publish his righteousness
for his lovingkindness endureth forever.

I wish they'd hurry.
I just got new glasses;
I guess I need remedial classes
because I still don't get the message,
I still don't believe I'm allowed to be:
the years turn and turn away
yet shames stay the same.
Let a voice come out of the heavens
saying Lo, or Yo,
I go before and prepare the way.
Or at least let the moon rise.
Or of these, a nice confluence.
Dear St. Lucy, pray for me
who apparently has only a virtual mind.
Plug me in or into me
where to think is to be unkind.

Apothecaries' Weight:
Twenty Brains Make One Scruple

Shaggy like a beard the shadow of the tree
On the longer deeper green made of grass.

Leaf spine turns a little beneath the butterfly.
Its name is cabbage white. No one loves it.

On the airplane level the woman says to me,
"As a family, we have been quite unlucky."

Some people's mere heads got hurt.
Little Other Boy got soap put deep.

Some people say, Well, what we do is nature, too.
Our thoughts like its hair grow out naturally.

Personally, I do not see anything as horrible as we
And really neither any general beauty

Like the longer deeper green.
If *cogito ergo sum* means

A Rwanda is a Rwanda is a Rwanda
Rape and Mr. Dahmer

Then not to know I think
Is no bad thing.

[continued]

But thinking, not to know
I think is bad.

Today, someone else tell.
Let the cabbage white eat gravity and green.

Abcedarium, Initial

Anthurium

First the ink is sheen on evening water
And across this land bridge
Traipse species that will eat or become
Cheese and ale and oil for a lamp,
The wick erect with a spathe of flame,
A flower of fuel powering the hand
That picks the pen and ruminates and writes.

E   The teeth of the comb

N   are fine as the hair

C   that lies along

O   the child's neck.

M   The smile of the baleen whale,

I   too,

U   is proof of god's

M   beneficence.

Molybdenum

It scares me that Primo Levi is dead.
How should I make shrift to hold out then,
whose deathcamp was secret and small?
I would set him a place at a different table,
removing every period but one—
the one with the spoon, the embryonic crawl
of the interrogative. Because not how
could it happen but that it did
leads to laws of gravity and pall.

Wisterium

caul. *arbeit. trauer.* trawl.
trowel. bird. worm. awl.
zygote. figure in a waistcoat.
wainscot. kitchen garden. dovecote.
beech bark. catkin. rude scrawl.
Hyperion, over all.

convolvulus. throat. thrall.
calyx. ether. anthem. sphere.
carnelian. corner. canter. queer.
cupola. cupboard. clapboard. dwell.

ell. ell. ell.

*Miss*ive

Where did words go?
I had them for you.

Similarly, the ink with which I addressed
my mess of envelopes has faded.
The letters are barely there.

I feel I am barely.
I've lit a candle for its little company.

I've looked at the light on the jade plant leaf.
It has dust, it has pores, it breathes.

Perhaps I have dust.
The candle has dust
and still it has light.

All right. OK,
for now.

Of Unknowing, The Cloud

In the morning would the white
cat nose the tall grass
along the driveway.

Careful not to touch, knowing
at a distance. Smell the synapse
as is the green thing springing
forth from the earth
also good to smell.

In the morning would the white
cat carefully
go its nose naming along
in the morning. It would, yes,
it did go. And in the morning watching
she thought this: it is important to remember
there is really no certain way
to be. What she wanted
to think is: I'm allowed.

Maybe

On the other hand, maybe you know everything there is to know and then some. Maybe the thumb is not for sucking, the lady not for burning. Maybe the next word is not going to come from the nice breast of the now turning world. Maybe there is no way out of here, maybe the next thing and the thing after it are both the ticking of the clock. Maybe it is sad enough in here to measure the levels on 1968's kneesocks.

Maybe tall buildings could crumble or should crumble. Maybe the dried petals could powder out of the book and you'd not even care, your heart having become the city where no tall buildings are and therefore a place without those shadows nurturing memory's fragrance so necessary for recognition which is to say love.

The heart beats, *I know, I know* and what it means is follow, follow, look for a sign. Once the stem of feathery grass pointed out the black rock where the ravens came to play and in their play let fall a feather and the severing sound of their wings threshing air—

O who cares, there is nothing to follow, there has never been a road. The ocean opens its flower in silence. No one comes. The stone stands in its shadow all day long, watching it come and go. *Maybe*, this is everything to know.

Persian Stanzas

How to advise those who, for a long time, believe stones are faithful? Love, grace saved from the censure of Great Day, do not deny me the names. I am a narrow vessel, a star asleep on its daybed. I have been such a long time in the night, your arc of tenderness a ploy, keeping me against the day when the inflection of the body should be entirely the late shrug of your shoulder, an accent too grave to alter the meaning of my sleep.

The good death is a package wrapped in somebody else's name. Give me your word you will send back all the stones to their places, all the stories, estuaries of water lilies, hyacinth all along the stairs' descent to childhood. A dead yellow dog and a bicycle pedal—wrap them back up. I have them already.

Tonight the night itself is a cross across which crosses are drawn. Yesterday I saw long the shadow of a young tree kept in the trunk of an older. What have I done? If only *every shadow entailed a sun*... Foregone; let the avenger pass over.

Rest in what menaces, heart. Call out the names. Let the traces of tears be the trees of salt that root the night sky. Call each root Star. Call each star Forgiveness. Call Forgiveness the diurnal fruit of Great Day.

Pro(verbial) (Re)creation in the Time of AIDS

A dog is barking behind me and I
think of its open mouth.
A wind lifts the leaves and they
shift like their own shadows.
A spider disturbed swings on its silk.

My new hat is full of dust.
It is dangerous
but I believe above me
I hear the tree making its leaves.
My heart burrs briefly.

The wasp measures the door and leaves.
Soon you'll come and open it.
When you do, some dogs will shut their mouths
thinking sometimes it is better
not to have had their day.

Exhibits A

Doubt is spun, a strand, it drifts, faint, and catches
A line is drawn across the field of vision
Crosswalk, double cross, valor, honor
Cross hairs in the gun sight, cheap talk
A fat cross man, a hot cross bun, a double lock

The sky a diagram, the eye a pentagon, milk fortified
On the exit ramp from the interstate, a shoe in the margin
The empty room, its door latch, catch in the throat
Gethsemene, the fool on the hill, the catch at Galilee
A shifting of the loaves, a floury light among the leaves

The way through the trees of his life blocked by a lion
The pendulum in his pants marks ample reasons
Dante's progress clocked by seasons
After the Fall the spider bobs the littlest bit
Silk stretches from star to pit

(Who) Didn't Think Right

And now, on your left, a little writing very little and so back to The Charming One, the star of so many fairy tales, accompanied by delightful hand signs. And now to The Lanky One and what on earth is he doing out there? (Here a brief problem-solving mode interferes: well, he could change places with _____.) And now? To continue with our tour, let's have a body instead of a wish. Whereupon there is an apprehension. There is concern certain parts are not presentable. Of which, oh dear, body parts on TV at the dinner table. Shades of Vietnam, strewn in an Indianan cornfield. Somehow the aerial view only is so unusual, so used to close-ups of newsworthy dismemberments (Maestro, footage of the Sarajevo market blown to smithereens, if you please) as we are. Orchestrated purveyors of suffering, sampling rather than surveying. Surveilling. Oops, here, via *la langue,* memory of The Supercilious One intrudes. A pox on your house, Mme. And now, back to (please don't say basics. Don't say our show, ether, please)—thank god for a typo, ether, there's a way out. *Enough and empty a way on through.* Bracing, refreshing, recuperative, essential, no—but it's something to quote oneself when of a mind to unknow.

(But unknowing, this is not what I had in mind, sir. Shit on sir. Ah, *bien*. Aaargh. Dirt be on your head. As it is on theirs? *As we forgive those who tresspass against us.* Not generally what mind has in mind. Ah, men.)

Varieties of Imperialist Experience

i.

It sounds like somebody's walking around on the roof.
I reckon it's falling clumps of snow.

Clumps of snow are walking around on the roof
for all I know.

Or knew, to be truthful.
Or, rather, exact.

ii.

Four months after a mystery illness struck her dumb
The Empress Michiko has spoken. The breakthrough came
on a state visit to a remote island in the Pacific.
The Empress watched a boy release
a small turtle into the sea. "When the next wave comes,
the turtle can return, no?" said she.

The Empress of Japan had collapsed from her illness
on her sixtieth birthday; it was said to be caused
by deep sorrow rumored to be caused
by a critical press. In the photo,
the Empress looks a bit like a turtle
about the head and neck.

iii.

Every teacher steals our waiting.
Body of work. Body of bliss. Island
vacation. Over
and over again, all roads end
in a trust in balance?
The never comfortable course of days,
the still stubborn stars—
how—despite teachers—substantial all this!
Plum blossom, sorrow, a special kind
of leaf, the place beyond serenity,
all rent-free. Struck suddenly
with something that must be joy
by coming across the footprints in snow
of a cat you know or hope to know.
Pebble under the snow
from an ocean you can only know
by what it did to what outlived it.
Let any opening moment turn
back into wanting again
and again. Briefly changed
from what we are
by a tourist tired
of snow's brochure.

What You Don't Know Won't Kill You

Today we are in a world whose ground crunches.
What do you know.

Also, either a bit of dust or a minute and tiniest bug
just landed on the frigid window sill
next to a nondescript slip of stem.
When your leaves are gone, it falls to another
to know you from what kind of stem you are.
And not to confuse you with a fuzzy—
which is to confirm that in the interim
the fuzzy flexed its wings and almost flew.
A tiniest gnat alone in the winter.
Hatched in the poinsettia, probably.
Does it know its world shouldn't be so cold?

For the sake of the poinsettia I forsake
the conservation of energy; each night,
to warm it, I give the thermostat a whirl.
Cold girl, her feet in a red foil pot of dirt,
but beautiful around the eyes
like the waitress in the diner last night.
Beautiful this world, too: there is green, there is blue,
and then there is snow. Pine, fir—
Oh.
The stem is pine straw.

[continued]

What will thrill you is what you no longer don't know.
No:

The gnat appears to be dying.
It clasps the proffered pine needle,
so I carry this stretcher over
and leave it on a poinsettia leaf,
hoping its death would be happier there.

From thinking of you, wherever you are,
no relief.

Saving the Appearances

On the way I see
the trees are glazed.
I open my mouth and breathe
to show them my vapor.

I did it to speak
the language of ice
or the language of white,
I don't have to know.

On the path, the prints
of animal feet.
A metrics of mammals
scanned by the snow.

Where being and being
seen coincide,
often the world
is cold.

For the sounds are other in Greek than in Latin, but the things are
neither Greek, nor Latin…

—St. Augustine, *Confessions*

Encode, *Enfilade*

And you who sleep in the vast rooms of dreams,
will you allow us one evening to read
those letters affixed to the walls
of one room? A crucifix

with its beautiful feet
might be an I, its text the object
of suffering's sliver: to work itself
out. Like the candle at your bedside now.

Homing In

Our Lady Of Perpetual Mildew is what I said to myself as I sat down. He shook it out then, the navy blue bathroom rug hung over the deck chair next to mine in hopes that it might dry. Nevertheless, it would mildew up there on the bathroom floor. It would mildew here on the deck chair arm. It was humid.

A robin walked in that armless way, the way calling attention to *look ma, no arms.* The neighbor riding his lawn mower whistled a tune. Both had rusty parts. A halo of gnats like a crown of thorns threatened to adorn me. I noted these things as I sat.

The neighbor began on the Andy of Mayberry theme. This deepened my sense of foreboding. Not inexplicably: It deepened it, belonging it did to the time I still lived in Brookhaven. (I like a sentence without that particular 'as,' excuse me.) Brookhaven, Brookhaven, Mississippi; "Homeseeker's Paradise," the sign said, planted in a triangle of always mown grass in front of a triangle of evergreen trees, Brookhaven, where I moved in 1968 and got little rectangle cards with two eyes from the Klan. Beneath the eyes, the Klan wrote We Are Watching You.

They were wasting their time.

Nothing might be comparable to that doleful era. Nothing might be but would be more relief.

Maybe after all it is a hymn he whistles; these neighbors are evangelicals of some stripe. Of some renown. Of some substance. (These last insinuate themselves, looking for an opening. I'll give them substance:

Wasps are affixing little paper lantern-like abodes inside all the window frames. The window screens don't fit. Some previous tenant's hapless efforts with duct tape make further efforts impossible. Maybe I made them. The screens, not efforts. I worked in the Keystone-Seneca Wire Cloth company and took my breaks in the metal cage in the factory's middle at three a.m. I see they've affixed one to the bough of this tree. Abode, not cage, not break, not factory. Here a noxious advertising tune begins in my brain: *(Burlington Coat Factory...* It's a danger to mention, a contagion, I hope you don't get it, don't know it, go through it, and now a word from our sponsors: *while)* while I wonder if this tree is a linden. I like the word. Otherwise, it, this tree, has sheaves or clusters of maple noses, but is not a maple. Do sheaves point up and clusters dangle down, exclusively? Not the sort of thing you ponder when working the night shift in the screen wire factory: our sponsors have changed their stripes.

[continued]

These halo-ing gnats may not be gnats. The one I flattened on my face went on, after flattening, as far as I can tell with a mirror, to suck my blood leaving, beneath a clot of painful scales, a tiny hickey-like affair. Maybe wasps eat them. The gnats, the may-be gnats, I mean. Did I say that before? I hoped it before. It may have been hope that drove me to pinch my own neck one weekend so that in the 8th grade Mississippi Monday someone would tease me about making-out, or in this case, necking. I hadn't the something to arrive at such desirable blotches by means of boys' mouths. Then. Thereafter, many mouths were affixed. Except Mikey's who was so shy he blew my bad girl cover so I blew him off. In a figurative sense. Some years later I learned he'd blown himself away.

The wasp enters its nest through its lantern hole. I always wanted to enter the squinty little eye of the penis just like that. Displaced person, displaced birth canal, displaced I.D., dunno about id. Imagine changing your gender, changing the deepest welts, those stripes. If I had one, I'd change to become a gay male. A gnat just flew into my eye.

Citronella candles neither deter nor discourage them, these gnats. I opened the box of Strike On Box matches upside down and they made a very pleasant sound as they scattered across the deck planks. Pick-up sticks should have been made out of wood. (I was, every time I was picked up.) This morning I caught the toaster oven on fire. (I've put the citronella candle on the arm of my chair.) Actually, the two pieces of not very good anyway bread caught on fire while I was upstairs praising and inspecting his cleaning of the bathroom. There is an arsonist around here, so the matches stuck between the deck planks worried me. You can't get good bread here.

The deck is rotting. Earlier in the month, wasps gnawed the deck furniture and now, transmuted, the deck furniture hangs from the branch of a tree and, as we have seen, turns my mind to a penis. Narrow-minded. One-track. My, my.

The semi-colon looks strange when you put the whole thing above the line. Some years ago, I stopped dotting my iyes, I mean my *i*'s (I have never used make-up). (That is a lie.) I have no idea why ("she swallowed the fly," another rhythm or rhyme looking for an opening; what opportunists these immortals be.) Now dotting an *i* looks Arabic, or Turkish, maybe, how should I know. But exotic. *Orientalizm*. East of the sun, west of the moon, another gnat bites the dust known as me.

The guy came to fix the gutter and deck at 7:30 a.m. Saturday, then he stomped around a while, slammed truck doors a while and left after an hour or so. He's been back and forth all day (it's still Saturday) and he whistled, too. It's going to rain. I am afraid when the gutter is fixed, the flapping about I hear in the wall of my room at night will stop. But this will not be good because I am afraid the flapping is the pair of blue birds I've seen sitting on our car antennae (one at a time) and that they have a nest and the eggs will hatch in the wall and there will be a terrible peeping and cheeping in the wall and bad dreams will ensue. I sublet my apartment to move in with him so where would I go? There's no *where to go*. So I'd have to knock a hole in the wall and then what? I'd have to look and know.

After all these months of planning, ever since I got here last week, he's been acting weird. He left angry, with his hood for graduation. He hasn't come back. It's been hours and hours. It is getting dark, it is going to rain, the gutter is fixed, the phone is ringing, the citronella candle spews factory smoke, the robin walks on the ant mound, armless. The trees have seen what is going to happen, the trees are holding their breaths. I'm mad because the cover to *The Web That Has No Weaver* has a stone-faced He feeding a spoonful to a slightly dismayed-looking She. It's more of the same. Nobody's whistling nothing now. Somebody's hammering something hard.

Märchen, Truckin'

We are sitting in our truck in Tivoli next to the laundromat where a load of whites hasn't made it to rinse yet and it occurs to us that this is the moment hoped for, referred to, suggested by, so many moments before when, reaching into the ashtray for turnpike change, my fingers were pricked like poor Rapunzel's lover by the thorns of a thousand upturned tacks. Well, a dozen. Diabolical, if someone thought it up, a spurned lover maybe, but I did it myself (goodbye, "we", contamination from *The New Yorker* pulled out of a recycling bin while waiting for other laundry to dry back in Boston); last things out of the apartment in Corrales, they've been riding around in the ashtray almost two years now. Once, hot and thirsty through Utah and Nevada all summer, I stuffed a rented car's ashtray so full of pits from the box of dates on which I'd spent the last of my food stamps, I couldn't get them out or close it when I returned it. They gave me my $300-no-credit-card-deposit back: they were either kind or had no eye for detail at the airport in Albuquerque. I guess I get to decide.

So it is the moment to pick out the tacks, practicing thereby the manual dexterity an aptitude test picked up twenty years ago in Atlanta but instead, as you can see, I've picked up my pen because all morning I've been hearing a voice saying something about *I, your own personal vision of loveliness...* and it was going to do something and say so but I forget what, so here I am in my truck on a Saturday morning in July, a sparrow yelling in the passenger side window, me writing on a 1950's notebook from a drugstore in 1970's Mississippi that features helpful, if obscure, tables on its pale yellow back cover (4 gills make 1 pint, 10 dollars make 1 eagle, 20 grains make 1 scruple), slipped under the steering wheel and balanced on my thigh, again with no or any where to go. I guess I get to decide.

I suppose it should have been Snow White with her finger pricked by a spindle and not Rapunzel with her lover lying with his eyes poked out in the briars below. But Snow White sickens, she's so sweet or Disneyfied, and the tower is one big prick, besides; these brambly blue words all look prickly, too, because last night, my true love was not true, and I'm afraid no other will blind my eyes.

Queen for a Day

One night in east Texas, a middle-aged woman with a shotgun walks into the 7-11 and announces she is going to kill herself. And first, everybody else.

It's different if you say, "*But* first..."

The cashier gets on the phone to 911 right quick and this is how anyone who wants to can know all about it: the TV show "Rescue 911." You can hear the woman hollering in the background of the cashier's call and him all tense and the calming dispatcher. You can see actual video footage interspersed with The Re-Enactment Of The Event.

It sounds like a sacrament.

Millions of police surround the 7-11, which is a small box. The TV screen is a box around the box and the re-enactment is a box around the footage of The Actual Event. The glass door of the 7-11 is the box where the shotgun woman will make the people kneel. But first a hostage woman comes flying out the door, into her car, and squeals away. She was in that 7-11 to pay for her gas and left her baby daughter in the car while she did, so the shotgun woman sets her free. At the time, it seems peculiar to me that she leaves. Why? I expect her to hunker down behind a patrol car and watch like me.

[continued]

Uh-oh, like life was TV.

So there they are, they are kneeling in a row, and you see the shotgun woman poking it in the back of a dark-haired woman's head. Then there is a blur of blue.

The next thing is a close-up of bony knees pulled up to a blue dress and heels sitting on the sidewalk outside the 7-11 right next to the door, his wig in his hands and police rushing past him into the 7-11 and the narrator tells us **this** is who wrestled the shotgun away and the shooter to the floor just as she was going to shoot.

They manage not to say "transvestite" by having his make-up be really bad in the re-enactment.

Imagine. There you are in Smalltown, Texas, with your wig off, on primetime TV, and there's the rest of your life in that box. Oh, hero everyday, opening it up to frame the heart's perfect shot.

About the Author

Liz Waldner is the author of *Dark Would (The Missing Person)*, *Etym(bi)ology*, *Self and Simulacra* (winner of the 2001 Beatrice Hawley Award), and *Homing Devices*. *A Point Is That Which Has No Part* was winner of the Iowa Poetry Prize and the Academy of American Poets Laughlin Prize for 2000. Her chapbooks include *Representation, Call, Read Only Memory, With the Tongues of Angels,* and *Memo (La)mento.* Her work has received The Poetry Society of America's Robert M. Winner award; grants from the Massachusetts Cultural Council, the Lannan Foundation/Centrum and The Barbara Deming Money for Women Fund; and fellowships from the Djerassi Foundation, Hedgebrook, Vermont Studio Center, and The MacDowell Colony, among others.

Ahsahta Press

SAWTOOTH POETRY PRIZE SERIES

GRAHAM FOUST, *Leave the Room to Itself*
AARON MCCOLLOUGH, *Welkin*

NEW SERIES

DAN BEACHY-QUICK, *Spell*
LISA FISHMAN, *Dear, Read*
PEGGY HAMILTON, *Forbidden City*
LANCE PHILLIPS, *Corpus Socius*
HEATHER SELLERS, *Drinking Girls and Their Dresses*
LIZ WALDNER, *Saving the Appearances*

MODERN AND CONTEMPORARY POETRY OF THE AMERICAN WEST

SANDRA ALCOSSER, *A Fish to Feed All Hunger*
DAVID AXELROD, *Jerusalem of Grass*
DAVID BAKER, *Laws of the Land*
DICK BARNES, *Few and Far Between*
CONGER BEASLEY, JR., *Over DeSoto's Bones*
LINDA BIERDS, *Flights of the Harvest-Mare*
RICHARD BLESSING, *Winter Constellations*
BOYER, BURMASTER, AND TRUSKY, EDS., *The Ahsahta Anthology*
PEGGY POND CHURCH, *New and Selected Poems*
KATHARINE COLES, *The One Right Touch*
WYN COOPER, *The Country of Here Below*
CRAIG COTTER, *Chopstix Numbers*
JUDSON CREWS, *The Clock of Moss*

H.L. DAVIS, *Selected Poems*

SUSAN STRAYER DEAL, *The Dark is a Door*

SUSAN STRAYER DEAL, *No Moving Parts*

LINDA DYER, *Fictional Teeth*

GRETEL EHRLICH, *To Touch the Water*

GARY ESAREY, *How Crows Talk and Willows Walk*

JULIE FAY, *Portraits of Women*

THOMAS HORNSBY FERRIL, *Anvil of Roses*

THOMAS HORNSBY FERRIL, *Westering*

HILDEGARDE FLANNER, *The Hearkening Eye*

CHARLEY JOHN GREASYBEAR, *Songs*

CORRINNE HALES, *Underground*

HAZEL HALL, *Selected Poems*

NAN HANNON, *Sky River*

GWENDOLEN HASTE, *Selected Poems*

KEVIN HEARLE, *Each Thing We Know Is Changed Because We
    Know It And Other Poems*

SONYA HESS, *Kingdom of Lost Waters*

CYNTHIA HOGUE, *The Woman in Red*

ROBERT KRIEGER, *Headlands, Rising*

ELIO EMILIANO LIGI, *Disturbances*

HANIEL LONG, *My Seasons*

KEN MCCULLOUGH, *Sycamore•Oriole*

NORMAN MCLEOD, *Selected Poems*

BARBARA MEYN, *The Abalone Heart*

DAVID MUTSCHLECNER, *Esse*

DIXIE PARTRIDGE, *Deer in the Haystacks*

GERRYE PAYNE, *The Year-God*

GEORGE PERREAULT, *Curved Like an Eye*

HOWARD W. ROBERTSON, *to the fierce guard in the Assyrian Saloon*

LEO ROMERO, *Agua Negra*

LEO ROMERO, *Going Home Away Indian*

MIRIAM SAGAN, *The Widow's Coat*

PHILIP ST. CLAIR, *At the Tent of Heaven*

PHILIP ST. CLAIR, *Little-Dog-of-Iron*

DONALD SCHENKER, *Up Here*

GARY SHORT, *Theory of Twilight*

D.J. SMITH, *Prayers for the Dead Ventriloquist*

RICHARD SPEAKES, *Hannah's Travel*

GENEVIEVE TAGGARD, *To the Natural World*

TOM TRUSKY, ED., *Women Poets of the West*

MARNIE WALSH, *A Taste of the Knife*

BILL WITHERUP, *Men at Work*

CAROLYNE WRIGHT, *Stealing the Children*

This book is set in Apollo type with Bauer Bodoni titles
by Ahsahta Press at Boise State University
and manufactured on acid-free paper
by Boise State University Printing and Graphics, Boise, Idaho.

AHSAHTA PRESS

2004

JANET HOLMES, DIRECTOR

SCOTT ABELS	JOHN OTTEY
J. REUBEN APPELMAN	ERICH SCHWEIKHER
SANDY FRIEDLY	AMY WEGNER
WENDY GREEN	MARY HICKMAN, INTERN
KAREN MOYER	AMY GARRETT, INTERN
BRANDON NOLTA	MIA WRIGHT, INTERN